Cookbook for Market Dominance and Shareholder Value

Standardising the Roles of Knowledge Workers

Cookbook for Market Dominance and Shareholder Value

Standardising the Roles of Knowledge Workers

Keith Sherringham

ATHENA PRESS
LONDON

COOKBOOK FOR MARKET DOMINANCE AND SHAREHOLDER VALUE
Standardising the Roles of Knowledge Workers
Copyright © Keith Sherringham 2005

All Rights Reserved

No part of this book may be reproduced in any form
by photocopying or by any electronic or mechanical means,
including information storage and retrieval systems,
without permission in writing from both the copyright
owner and the publisher of this book.

ISBN 1 84401 466 5

First Published 2005 by
ATHENA PRESS
Queen's House, 2 Holly Road
Twickenham TW1 4EG
United Kingdom

Printed for Athena Press

This document is for information purposes only and any advice given is of a general nature only and may not be applicable to an individual or a specific situation. The author accepts no responsibility for any consequential loss or damage arising from the use of this document.

Acknowledgments

Many people contributed to this book and the ideas over the years. My sincerest thanks to them all. In formulating the ideas many discussions were held with Pat McConnell and Douglas Bell and they provided many valuable insights and support.

The manuscript was read and improved by Robert Thomas, Andrew Symaniz and Jean Grayson.

Special thanks to Jean and Michael Grayson for their loving support over the years.

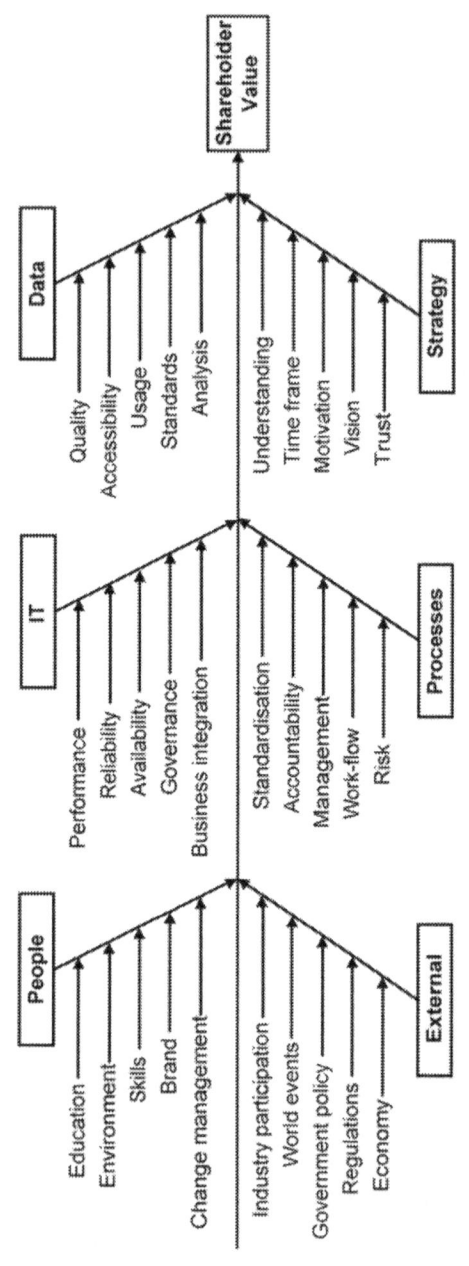

Factors impacting on shareholder value.

About this Cookbook

Introduction

Seldom does a book quite like this come across your desk. Looking for a good read? Wanting to put a new perspective on things? Need a refreshing approach to some old business issues? Then keep reading. Some of your preconceptions may be challenged, whilst others may be clarified.

Whether you are looking for practical steps to follow or for the big picture, then there is plenty here to challenge you. Be sure to take notes and/or underline or highlight as you go through.

Getting the most from the cookbook

Realising the value of this cookbook rests with you. We hope you will read it from end to end and get the big picture. You can also opt to read one section at a time to gain a clear view of the detail or, if you prefer, you can read one recipe at time. Either way, take your time and enjoy.

The sections are:

- Where are we now? – Gain perspective and take a moment to reflect.

- Savouring the Sensations – Whet your appetite and get the basics before going on to reap the rewards from the recipes.

- Process Perfection – Wondering what work-flow can do for you? Peruse and pursue the practical processes that perform for you.

- Data Management Delights – Dare to savour these delicacies. Discover for yourself how easy it is.

- Tantalising Technology – Taste the true temptations. Take the trophy. It is time to take on technology and triumph through these trusted tactics.

- Internet Interactivity – Initiate the innovations that the Internet brings.
- Optimised Outsourcing – Oh to be rid off those opulent outsources and to be back in control of your business. Read the recipes and reap the rewards.
- Forward to the Future – For those that favour the future, many opportunities and rewards await. Are you the one for market dominance?

Perspective

As shareholders and taxpayers, we have seen the good and the extravagant within business and government. Over time, I have come to realise that the principles of standardisation and the application of assembly line techniques can be applied to all areas of business and that these are the keys to guaranteed service delivery and lower costs. Within business, these proven principles have been successfully applied to everything from making Subway sandwiches to the production of wine and the manufacture of the most complicated consumer goods. In fact, these same techniques have been successfully applied to every area of business endeavour except the roles of knowledge workers[1] and their associated Information Technology (IT).

Inevitably, the question arose – "is the failure to apply these proven principles to knowledge workers the reason why hidden costs are increasing and service cannot be guaranteed?" This led to a second question – "can the application of these proven principles stem the ongoing failings of and the underperformance of IT?"

YES! Was the answer I kept getting to these questions.

Further consolidation of this view came with the Internet and the mirroring of the disorganised knowledge worker operations on websites and other e-business activities. The absence of proven business processes, the lack of work-flow, and the inability to find information on websites led me to ask – "Why were all the same

---

[1] Knowledge workers collate dispersed information and present it to customers to resolve issues.

mistakes being made again?" In the intervening period little has changed in this regard.

I finally decided that the way to stimulate the ideas of standardisation and the application of assembly line techniques to the roles of knowledge workers and to address the fundamental failings of IT, was to write a set of recipes. After all, this is what we are arguing. People look for standards, techniques, principles and recipes to follow.

Taking the proven concepts from other areas of business endeavour, the concepts of part management and assembly line techniques are applied to the roles of knowledge workers to show how to:

- lower costs;
- guarantee service delivery;
- stop the ongoing waste of money on Information Technology (IT);
- return shareholder value;
- better the workplace.

Whether you are a shareholder wondering why costs keep increasing or a taxpayer frustrated with government waste, or a CEO under pressure from shareholders, or a rising star looking for that something special, I trust that you find these recipes of use.

The ultimate reason for writing this book is that I wanted to share these ideas with people for the betterment of humanity.

I leave it to you to benefit from them.

Contents

About this Cookbook — ix
Introduction — ix
Getting the most from the cookbook — ix
Perspective — x

Where are we now? — 17

Savouring the Sensations — 22
Recipes Rule — 23
Recipes for Business — 24
  Branding — 24
  Marketing — 24
  The Media — 24
  Media Handling — 24
  Sales — 25
  Warehousing — 25
  Apply All Areas — 25

Recipe Dominance — 26
Audience – Task – Recipe — 28
Kinds of Knowledge Worker — 30
  Producers — 30
  Creators — 30

Process Perfection — 31
Continuous Customer Centric — 32
Marvels of Modelling — 34
Concept Creation and Cultural Change — 35
  Choosing the Couch — 35
  Targets to Shoot at — 35
  The Power of the Three — 36

Premium Process Positioning — 37
Education Edification — 38

Work-flow Wanted	39
Sexy Six-Sigma	40
Multiple Product Manufacturing	42
Data Management Delights	**43**
Wisdom Wanted	44
Boardroom Balance	46
Seven Steps	47
Accessions	48
Transfer	48
Data Laundry	48
Quality Control	49
Documentation	49
Archiving	49
Making Information Available to Users	49
Information Relationships	50
Sustainable Simplicity	51
Expectation Management	51
Priority Management	51
Actionable Monitoring	52
Communication	52
Cultural Change	52
Role of IT	53
Easy and Business Integrated	53
Tantalising Technology	**54**
Boardroom Balance	56
Defining the Driver	58
The IT Assembly Line	59
A-grade Architecture	60
Consolidated Data Storage and Access	62
Information Presentation and Delivery	64
Migration Mitigation	66
Organised Outsourcing	68
Precision Parts	69

Internet Interactivity — **70**

   Wondrous Websites — 71
   Internet Integration — 73
   Intranet – Internet Inclusion — 74

Optimised Outsourcing — **75**

   Securing Strategy — 76
   Preventing Problem Passing — 77
   Owning Ownership — 78
   Intellectual Property Intern — 79
   Accountant Accountability — 80
   Business Process Bonds — 81
   Reward-Based Returns — 82
   Dependency Through Empowerment — 83
   Breaking the Relationship — 84

Forward to the Future — **85**

Where are we now?

Whether it is Subway sandwiches, McDonald's fast food, Nokia mobile phones, Mercedes cars, LG fridges or a drink of Guinness, the proven principles of standardisation, parts management, work-flow and assembly line techniques have been successfully applied. Indeed, these principles are used daily in all areas of business endeavour except the roles of knowledge workers.

In many organisations, knowledge workers now dominate the workforce. Whether it is customer service representatives, sales consultants or financial analysts, knowledge workers take information from different areas, collate it and present it back to clients. The roles of knowledge workers are characterised by:

- failure to guarantee service delivery;
- lack of work-flow and systematic organisation;
- duplication of effort;
- ongoing re-creation of information when it should not be necessary;
- increasing hidden costs;
- failure of Information Technology (IT) systems to deliver better results;

> **We know that:**
>
> - If you keep doing the same things you get the same results;
> - Standardisation and the application of assembly line techniques lowers costs, guarantees service delivery, creates market dominance and returns shareholder value;
> - Ignorance is where you don't know better but stupidity is where you know better and keep doing it!

- near absence of standardisation;
- high risk operations;
- poor accountability.

Contrast the above to a production line where companies know exactly the number of people required to produce a known quantity to a known quality. Many organisations do not know how many knowledge workers they have, nor what they are producing, at what cost.

If you were to take the roof off a company and look at the knowledge workers, then you would probably see something like Figure 1.

The customer approaches an organisation and deals with one customer service representative, who queries multiple back-end systems to answer the question. The representative may not find what they want, so they have a discussion with a co-worker, who tries to do the same thing and brings in another co-worker. In the meantime, the customer gets frustrated and approaches another representative who goes through the same process. Add to this the duplication between Internet and Intranet, disparate websites and the sending of e-mails that end up on the floor and the customer asks – "How does the place function?" or "Why do I waste my time with them?"

Ask your customer if this is funny...

If Boeing's assembly line produced the Mumbo instead of the Jumbo (Figure 2), it would be in trouble. If airlines flew the Mumbo instead of the Jumbo they would go bankrupt. Yet knowledge workers often produce and fly the Mumbo.

Where are we now?

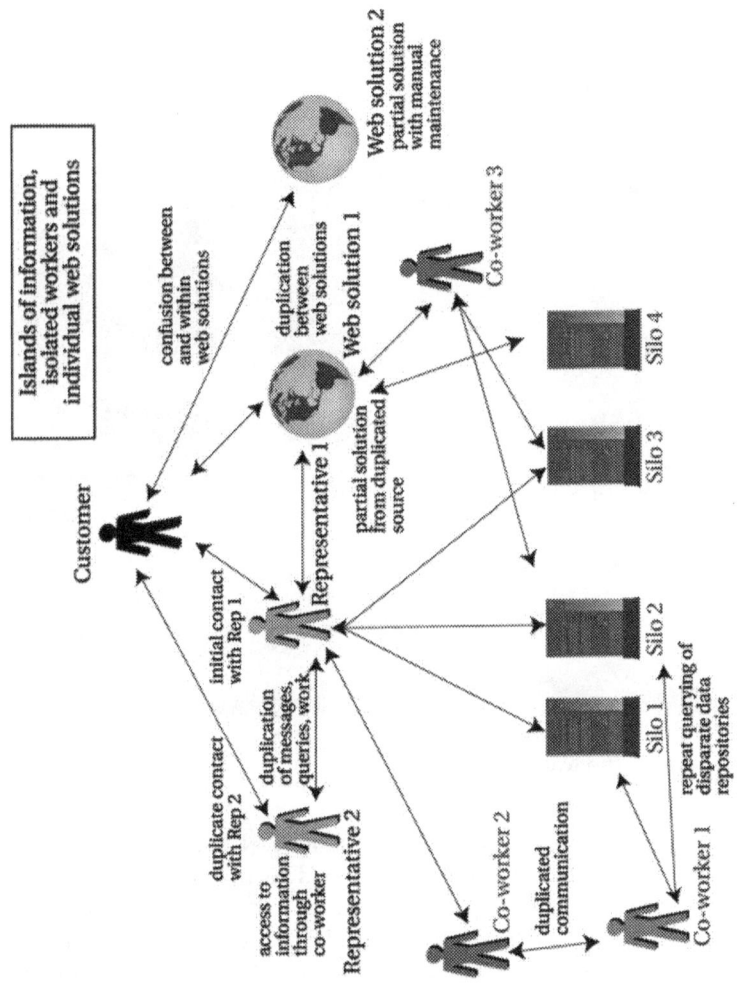

Figure 1. Knowledge workers who deliver higher costs and poor service.

Despite all of the books, journals, and thousands of column inches given over to business efficiency, information on the application of standardisation and assembly line techniques to the roles of knowledge workers receives little coverage.

Figure 2. The Mumbo Jet.

The sceptic will say it cannot be done. Well, they said the same when standardisation was first applied to manufacturing. When these principles were applied to fast food, they said the same. Yet history shows us that it only needs one to do it, to gain the competitive advantage, and for it to be accepted as the industry standard (Figure 3). History also shows us that the change will be resisted but one visionary will persist and be successful.

Are you going to be the one that transforms your knowledge workers?

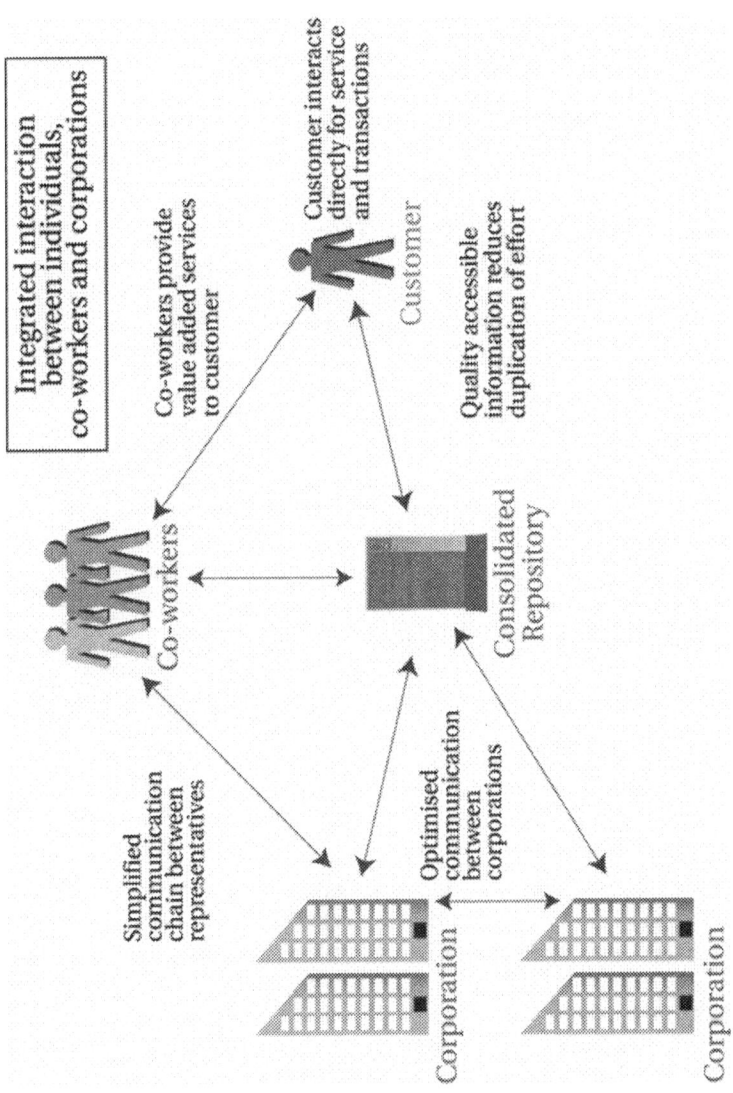

Figure 3. The knowledge worker production line to lower costs and guarantee service delivery.

Savouring the Sensations

We know how to run our businesses but when are we going to stop being held to ransom by Information Technology (IT)?

The need to lower costs, guarantee service delivery, increase market share, profitability and stronger brand recognition form the basis of modern business. The steps required to achieve these have been the subjects of voluminous copy, and yet the basic principles are often overlooked and/or ignored.

Some of the best manufacturers in the world routinely apply parts management, assembly line techniques and standardisation to the production side of their business, but for some reason, these principles are considered not to apply to knowledge workers.

When it comes to Information Technology (IT) the situation is even worse. IT is often considered to be beyond these proven business principles.

> **Key Ingredients**
>
> - A belief that IT and knowledge workers are subject to the same rules as the rest of business;
> - A willingness to apply proven principles to IT and knowledge workers.

In this cookbook you will see that everything is a recipe and that these proven business principles can be applied to the last great area of hidden costs and inefficiency, that of IT and the role of the knowledge workers.

With all of the books, journals, and courses on business, and the millions of dollars spent on business consultants, can lower costs and increased shareholder value be as simple as a set of recipes in a book? YES! Undoubtedly. The history of business shows this, but like the baking of bread, it is only as good as the implementation.

Recipes Rule

Every process is a recipe that can be duplicated.

Across the world, every day of the week, millions of people bake bread. There are many different types of bread and yet so many people, of all levels of skill, can consistently produce any style of bread. We all know that there is no magic to this and that the reason for this is very simple – all these people follow a RECIPE.

In a recipe, the series of steps necessary to achieve an outcome are detailed in sequence, together with what is required at each step. It is that simple!

From the manufacture of cars through to the flipping of hamburgers, sale of real estate and the payment of accounts, all aspects of business require a series of processes to be completed in sequence with the required information/parts available at each step, i.e. every business process is a recipe!

Recipes for Business

Recipes apply to all areas of business and in any business. The argument about uniqueness and that recipes cannot be applied is a myth!

Branding

There are standard principles for branding, brand creation and brand recognition. There are standard laws (recipes) that apply to all brands in any business type. There are standard ways of destroying a brand as well.

Marketing

This area of business often seems to be dominated by touchy-feely concepts and is often seen as black magic. The reality, however, is that there is a series of basic rules for successful marketing. When these rules are applied, marketing is successful for a wide range of products and services in a diverse range of industries.

The Media

When Rupert Murdoch was busy building his global media empire, he was famed for using formulas for his newspapers. The *Sun* newspaper in London is seen as a classic example of this. So successful has his approach been, that around the world everything from magazines to newspapers to TV shows are produced to formulas.

Media Handling

There are books, consultants and training courses galore that tell you how to handle the media. They tell you how to not answer questions, how to turn questions to your advantage, how to control the interviewer, how to use 30-second sound-bites and more. These are all recipes.

Sales

There are basic activities to do for increasing sales e.g. advertising, consistency, persistency, follow-through with customers etc. There are hundreds of books on sales and they keep identifying the core competencies and activities – they give you recipes.

Warehousing

The basics of warehousing and stock control are parts management and work-flow. This principle has been around since way before the use of IT, when everything was recorded with pen and paper.

Warehousing functions smoothly and seamlessly because standard recipes are used and followed.

Apply All Areas

Fact: recipes apply to all areas of business activity and can be used to guarantee service delivery across all aspects of the enterprise. The information presented and the positioning and packaging may differ but at the end of the day, recipes rule and there is no reason why they should not be systematically applied to the roles of knowledge workers. It is a matter of belief!

Recipe Dominance

Recipes create market dominance. Benefit from being the de facto market standard.

Whether it is food processing, manufacturing, cleaning or retail, the global business environment is dominated by major players within each market. The success of these companies is due to many things but at the end of the day, they have the following attributes in common:

- Brand recognition as the market leader;
- Guaranteed service delivery;
- The de facto industry standard;
- Developed, and/or own, and/or implemented the standard recipes for their market.

Of all of these, it is standard recipes that deliver the others, together with the added benefit of the ability to lower costs.

Yes, that is right! By having a standard set of recipes a business can guarantee service delivery, can lower costs and become the de facto market standard. Once you are the de facto market standard, you create market dominance. The examples are numerous and include:

Category	*Company*
Software	Microsoft
Hamburgers	McDonald's
Aeroplanes	Boeing
Microchips	Intel

Category	*Company*
Mobile Phones	Nokia
Cars	Ford
Watches	Rolex
Overnight parcels	FedEx

Across the world, McDonald's can guarantee service delivery. A Big Mac in Hong Kong is the same as a Big Mac in Sydney and the same as a Big Mac in New York. McDonald's is famous for designing, implementing and owning the business processes (recipes) for standardised fast food franchises.

McDonald's success is based on:

- standard presentation;
- standard tools;
- standard procedures;
- standard parts;
- standard information;
- standard training;
- standard assembly line techniques;
- standardised quality assurance;
- standardised accountability.

Figure 4. Guaranteed quality around the world.

Above all, McDonald's uses standard recipes for many aspects of their business. This standardisation of their operations and their adherence to recipes is why McDonald's is the de facto market standard for fast food franchises and have market dominance.

The ability of Burger King to replicate the model (copy and follow the recipes) is why it is successful and is second in the marketplace. The ability of KFC, Red Rooster and Domino's etc. to apply these recipes to different food groups is why they are the market leaders in their selected categories.

Henry Ford had the vision to create the assembly line for cars. Now we are told that you cannot bring assembly line techniques and standardisation to the roles of knowledge workers. Yet history shows it takes one visionary to do it and to become the de facto standard.

Will you be the Henry Ford of knowledge workers?

Audience – Task – Recipe

For any recipe to be successful, the recipe has to be applied in context.

Within business, a recipe is related to a task and the task is conducted because of the need to meet the expectations of an audience. This leads to the Audience – Task – Recipe structure.

Consider the sales process. Whether it is the selling of a movie ticket, a house or consulting service, the Audience – Task – Recipe approach applies. Audience is a customer, the task is to sell them something and the recipe contains the steps needed and information required in sequence to achieve the required outcome. This is exactly the same as the need to bake bread to feed the family.

Within each task, a series of additional recipes may be required for a given step, e.g. the need to grind the flour may be omitted if prepared flour is provided, just as billing and payment details are needed in the sales process.

The Audience – Task – Recipe concept can be applied to any business, area or activity, and it allows for standardisation by audience and task. Consider the task of selling a chair to both wholesale and retail customers. Whilst the task is the same, the audience is different. The recipe may be the same (or different) but different information is required at some of the steps, e.g. pricing and discounts.

The power of the recipe lies in the ability to guarantee service

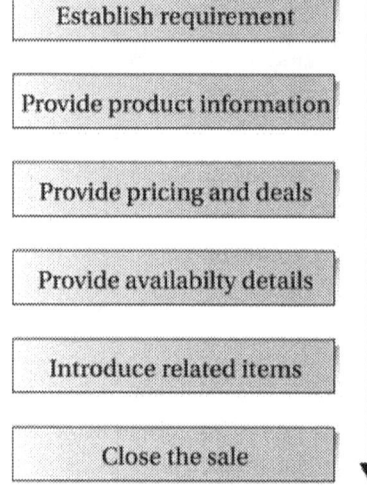

Figure 5. A recipe of the sales process.

delivery. Consider the sale of a mobile phone. Additional revenue and customer satisfaction is achieved through the sale of insurance, faceplates, hands-free kits, batteries, chargers, etc. By having a standard recipe that anyone can follow, with the appropriate information provided at each step, the maximum value for each sale can be effectively and efficiently realised by having people follow the recipes.

Whether an item is being purchased in a shop, sold over the phone, or acquired over a website, the Audience – Task – Recipe approach works across the different channels and mediums.

Kinds of Knowledge Worker

Despite the diverse variety of knowledge workers, recipes apply to all knowledge worker roles.

There are two main types of knowledge workers: producers and creators. Both roles can benefit from the use of recipes and the associated information management and work-flow.

Producers

These knowledge workers are the backbone of the business and produce the goods.

Whether it is selling real estate, solving customer enquiries or settlement of accounts, these employees go through the same recipes each time. The positioning and packaging may differ and the information needed may vary but the steps involved are essentially the same.

These roles are heavily recipe driven and continuously repeat the recipes.

Creators

These knowledge workers tend to do something once and are not associated with production. This is where by doing things for the first time and establishing how things work, the mistakes are made. Examples include those associated with new systems implementations, designers, pioneers of new business etc.

Even though these knowledge workers tend to do things once, they still use recipes for many parts of their business and can benefit from organised information management and work-flow. They often create the recipes for others.

Process Perfection

Even a Subway sandwich is made using assembly line techniques and yet the knowledge workers remain untouched.

Work-flow is at the heart of a modern assembly line because it is the most effective, the most efficient, and guarantees service delivery.

On an assembly line, the different people perform different roles and don't need to worry about where the parts come from. The design of the assembly line ensures that they just get the right parts at the right time, i.e. the parts come to the people.

Contrast this with knowledge workers, who need intimate knowledge of:

- where information is stored;
- what application the information is stored in;
- how to get the information;
- where to use it in the process.

What is even worse is that the knowledge workers:

- have varying capabilities;
- go to the parts;
- collect the parts one at a time;
- create multiple instances of a part (copy and paste) when there should be no need to.

The cost of NOT doing work-flow and recipes is greater than the cost of implementation. Currently, we do NOT account for those hidden costs.

Continuous Customer Centric

Customer interaction drives the business and its processes.

Many people that I speak to agree with the concepts of and the need for work-flow and assembly line techniques for knowledge workers. They often say "we used to have something similar before computers!" Many have small-scale implementations, e.g. check lists and sign-off, but I am often asked where to start and how not to be daunted by the changes required.

> **Productivity Tips**
>
> - Use customer centric work-flow to deliver results for customers;
> - Small steps in a sensible way;
> - Keep it simple.

As with all things, focus on the customer and look at how the customer interacts with an organisation. Drive the exercise by meeting the needs of the customer.

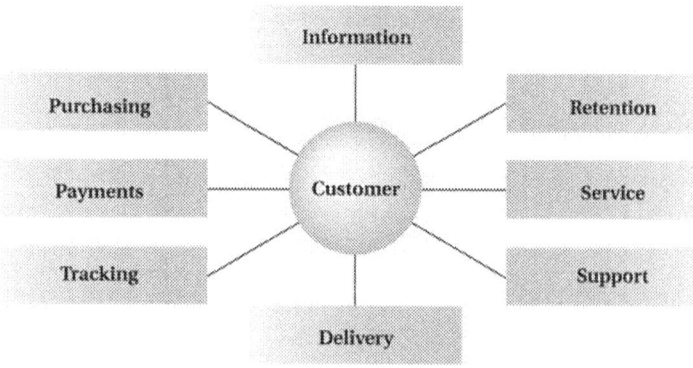

Figure 6. The customer wants to interact with all parts of the business and the customer is not concerned with internal structure.

Do things in small steps, in a sound and sensible way (Figure 7). Avoid the big bang and the vain hope that it would all work out if only they just did it in one particular way. People have an infinite capacity to avoid things that do not work for them. Keep it simple.

Ingredients	Instructions
Identification of customer interaction with the business	1) Take one area of business from end-to-end and determine how the customer interacts.
Analysis of business processes required to support customer needs	2) Establish the work-flow and recipes required to meet the customer needs at each point of interaction.
Practical implementation with a customer focus	3) Apply in a systematic and sensible way with a focus on customer needs and expectations.
	4) Extend to other areas of business.

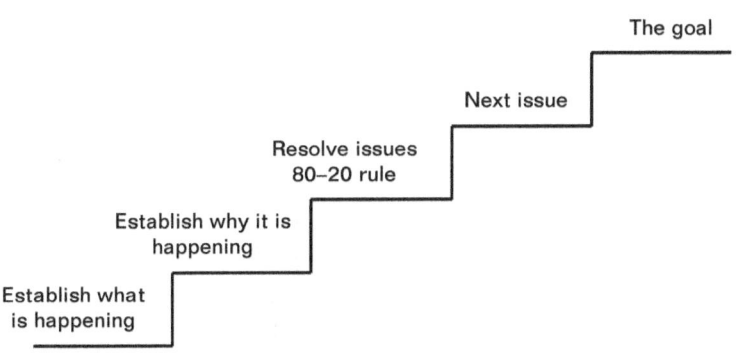

Figure 7. Process to realising the goal.

Marvels of Modelling

The operation of any assembly line can be modelled, monitored and optimised.

Since the assembly line was first adopted, work-flow has been modelled, optimised and monitored. Within manufacturing there is a plethora of software that is routinely used for this. When it comes to knowledge workers, the assembly lines are seldom designed, rarely optimised and effective and efficient monitoring is almost absent.

The practice of many business analysts of drawing boxes and defining a work-flow is not enough. There is no focus on handling exceptions and on quality of hand-off. If you actually talk to the workers at the coalface (frontline) and ask them "where do you get this?", "where does this go?" and model the results, amazing insights are found. You will be told everything that is wrong, everything that is right and exactly what they want. The assembly line is not about imposing a solution but taking the expertise that is there and harnessing it.

Ingredients	Instructions
Workers who can spend some time away from production	1) Using the expertise of the coalface workers, have the analysts discover what information is sourced where and passed on to whom.
Analysts with excellent communication skills and the ability to project	2) Model the work-flow described using simulation software.
Simple work-flow simulation software	3) Peer review with coalface workers.
	4) Ongoing use of the models for optimisation and monitoring.

Concept Creation and Cultural Change

Leverage the ability of people to choose and criticise when driving cultural change.

With knowledge worker optimisation and the application of assembly line techniques, the issues of concept creation and cultural change come to the fore.

Choosing the Couch

The ability to conceptualise is a skill that is not universally available. People can walk into a furniture store and choose between three couches, but getting them to articulate beforehand what they want is often very difficult.

The number of times people have tried to design systems and IT solutions for knowledge workers only to see them fail is phenomenal. The reality is that people can choose between options but often find it hard to articulate and conceptualise. Whilst the need to build three couches is often a time-consuming and frustrating process, it is often the best way to get results and quickly.

Targets to Shoot at

The extension of the "choosing the couch" principle is the "target to shoot at" approach. We all know that it is easier for people to deconstruct things than it is to construct them. People find it much easier to take something that is there and tell you everything that is wrong with it. People find it hard to propose and create an alternative. This is seen in everything from the criticism of politicians through to food tasting in restaurants.

When driving cultural change, you are asking for things from people and you are asking them to do things differently. When you want something from someone, you need to make it as easy as possible for them to do it for you.

The "target to shoot at" approach involves trying to understand what people want and creating a target for them to shoot at (deconstruct). The target has to be good enough to get their buy-in and support but bad enough that they can pick holes in it and take ownership. If the target is too good, then it is seen as a solution that is being forced upon them with only lip service being paid to their concerns and needs. For cultural change to succeed there must be ownership of issues and problem resolution at source.

By putting up a series of targets to shoot at, the process of defining requirements, cultural change and ownership is realised. As time goes by, the amount of effort required for the targets becomes less and the gap between targets becomes less.

Like choosing couches, the process of putting up targets to have them ripped down can be frustrating but is often the only way to realise the change.

The Power of the Three

The "power of the three" is often seen as one of the most effective and efficient strategies for driving cultural change. The power of the three comes from having one with the vision and the strategy, one with the ability to manage the details and aspects of the day-to-day implementation and one to address the sales and politics.

Together they form a powerful combination. These groups of three work together in all areas and at all levels of an organisation to drive the cultural change. These groups work in the business by setting examples for the others to follow.

Premium Process Positioning

Business process development is NOT dependent upon IT.

Perhaps one of the most significant advances in business optimisation was the implementation of "just-in-time ordering". Whilst the use of IT and computers facilitated the adoption of this methodology, just-in-time ordering can be achieved using human resources alone.

The reality of process evolution driving business optimisation without the need for IT is counter to the common perception.

> **Productivity Tip**
>
> Advances in business process are not dependent upon new IT.

Ingredients

Identification of business processes

Understanding of IT application

Practical application of IT to meet a business need

Instructions

1) Establish a clear understanding of how the business operates and the processes involved.

2) Review IT developments in terms of optimisation of the work-flow and business practices.

3) Develop detailed business cases, including cost savings and risk analysis.

4) Apply IT solutions as required to optimise business based on sound business principles.

Education Edification

Training programs need to allow for the change in mindset in moving from production to problem solving.

The ongoing training and skilling of staff is an important business activity. With the adoption of automation and technology, the role of the operative changes from that of production to that of solving problems when things go wrong, i.e. an autopilot flies a plane but the pilot intervenes when things go wrong. The operative moves to higher value activities. This change of skills applies to assembly lines and particularly to knowledge workers.

Problem diagnosis prescription and remedy is a higher-value skill set that is not always inherent to those who specialise in production. The challenge is to accommodate this change within human capital management programs.

Ingredients

Institutional and employees values framework

Re-skilling program

Re-training program

Incentives and corrections

Cultural change program

Instructions

1) Using the values framework and employee-profiling present in many companies, identify those that are suited to higher end value-adding problem-solving.

2) Facilitate the development of these resources through re-skilling and training with the appropriate incentives and corrections.

3) For production skilled personnel, use cultural change programs, together with re-skilling and re-training.

4) Ongoing support and human capital investment.

Work-flow Wanted

Software development needs to move from more features with increasing complexity, to simplified work-flow.

Software is increasing in complexity. More and more features are being added to software to be used by fewer and fewer people. Furthermore, software is designed to be feature driven instead of work-flow driven.

Whilst feature-driven applications are fine for generic activities, e.g. word processing and spreadsheeting, many roles and jobs are task specific. Consider the signing of an agreement. Copies and letters need to be sent to named parties, results recorded for billing and reporting etc. That is, once an activity is completed in sequence, a series of other ones need to be completed. Many times, we rely upon human memory to do these things when the tasks should be auto-generated by the application.

Ingredients

An understanding of business processes

List of recipes

Business and work-flow modelling

Performance monitoring and reporting

Instructions

1) For one area of business, develop the required recipes.

2) Conduct business and work-flow modelling for verification and optimisation.

3) Develop applications that are work-flow driven and/or implement interfaces to the existing applications that are work-flow driven.

4) Ongoing performance monitoring, with regard to reduced error rates.

5) Repeat for all aspects of the business.

Sexy Six-Sigma

Quality and performance-driven monitoring of knowledge workers through measurement of customer interaction.

Quality assurance has been addressed in many ways with differing degrees of success. The latest of these is Six-Sigma, which has been successfully used by the likes of General Electric to ensure quality within manufacturing.

Like Total Quality Management (TQM), Six-Sigma is currently the flavour of the month and there is a whole vocabulary around it. A simple User Requirements document now has a whole new tenor associated with it. Similar to TQM, the intent of the exercise (the important part) looks like being lost in the application. Just as TQM became another box-ticking exercise, so Six-Sigma is heading the same way.

There have been few initiatives to apply Six-Sigma to the roles of knowledge workers. Those that have tend to become lost in the detail.

The challenges with Six-Sigma are:

- to choose the parts of the process that are important;
- the selection of a meaningful level of operation for measurement and reporting;
- the complexity of implementing it to the role of the knowledge worker;
- recognition of affordable Six-Sigma.

A practical approach to Six-Sigma for knowledge workers is to look at the key part of the process, the interaction with the customer, and focus on this.

For a given level of cost, apply Six-Sigma to customer interaction at key points of the business. Whilst the use of Six-Sigma can be extended subsequently, this focus:

- is readily definable;
- can be easily measured;

- allows failures to be quickly identified;
- ensures that if the customer is satisfied, the rest of the system works for now.

Ingredients	Instructions
Recognition of key customer groups	1) For the business, identify key customers both internal and external.
List of key deliverables for customers	2) Identify key deliverables for the customers and the acceptable level of quality delivery for a stated cost.
What-if scenario modelling for optimisation	
Routine performance monitoring	3) Initiate routine performance monitoring at the key points for key customers.
Actionable reporting	4) Follow though with actionable managerial reporting.
	5) Conduct what-if scenario modelling to improve performance.
	6) Extend to additional areas of the business.

Multiple Product Manufacturing

Multi-branded products often come off one product assembly line. There is a great opportunity to apply the same principle to knowledge workers.

Manufacturing has identified further cost savings and optimisation through the use of multiple product manufacturing. The same assembly line that turns out one brand of baked beans also turns out other brands of baked beans.

From the canning of food through to the manufacture of complex outboard engines, multiple product manufacturing has been successfully used across a range of products and industries.

The ability to apply multiple product manufacturing principles to the roles of knowledge workers is significant. Consider banking. For foreign exchange trades, cash settlements, mortgages and many other areas of operation, the banks are required to send almost the same information between institutions. Through having the banks share one common set of technology to support the processing of the transactions, banks can realise significant cost savings and ensure guaranteed service delivery.

The potential rewards from the application of multiple product manufacturing to the roles of knowledge workers is huge. Opportunities abound for both those supplying the production line and those using it.

Data Management Delights

Make no mistake, data management is a business imperative and is a simple and cost effective exercise.

Data management is such a humble and overlooked activity and yet the failure to manage data efficiently and effectively is one of the key reasons for escalating hidden costs and poor customer service.

At the most basic level, an organisation functions as follows (BIDS):

Brains + Infrastructure + Data = Services

In business we sell services (products) for a profit. These services are produced by our people (brains) using resources such as desks, computers, and plant and equipment (infrastructure). To make it all happen, they need the right data (information).

In many organisations considerable time and effort is spent creating, monitoring, managing and ensuring brains, services and infrastructure. However, data management often receives scant attention.

> **Productivity Tips**
>
> - Data management is not a luxury, it is a business necessity;
> - The cost of NOT managing data is greater than the cost of doing it. The cost is currently NOT accounted for.

Effective and efficient data management underpins all aspects of business. The recipes that are the lifeblood of business are themselves data. To implement the recipes, the data has to be presented at the right time in the right way.

Whether it is the manufacture of a washer or a Boeing 747, the entire production line is dependent upon not only the right flow of parts but also the timely availability of correct data.

Wisdom Wanted

The goal is wisdom management. Knowledge management is just another diversionary trend and continues to fail because of a lack of data management.

Whilst knowledge management is a current buzzword within business and many millions of dollars are spent trying to achieve it, much of the effort is misplaced.

First of all it is wisdom (power/profit) access and management that is required. Wisdom management relies upon that most humble of activities – data management (Figure 8).

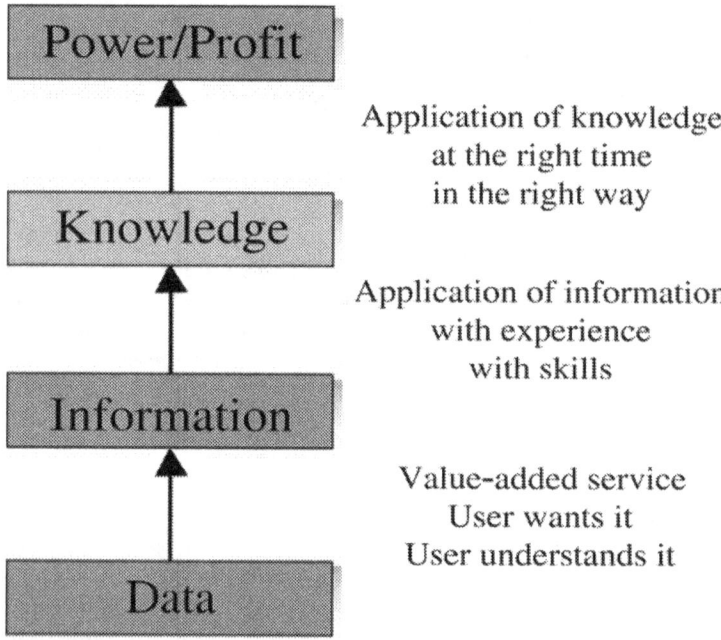

Figure 8. Realisation of wisdom/power/profit starts with data management.

Data Management Delights

Data are the "raw numbers" or "raw text", so to speak. Data often exists in a variety of formats in different applications and in paper-based hard copy.

Data only becomes information when it is in a format that a user wants and understands. A financial report can be produced through a value-adding process, but if a user does not understand it or does not want to know about it, then that report is just data.

Information comes from a value-adding process of taking data and presenting it at the right time, in the right way, to the right audience.

> **Have You Considered?**
>
> - The tracking and management of profits and expenditure is a data management activity.
> - Anyone not doing this would be seen as ludicrous.

Knowledge comes from the combination of experience, information and skills.

Power/profit/wisdom comes from the application of knowledge at the right time, in the right way.

By first addressing data management, information management can be conducted, then knowledge management and finally the management of wisdom can be achieved.

Contrary to what many people perceive, we live in a world of data overload, NOT information overload.

Boardroom Balance

With leadership and resourcing, things happen. Data management does not occur by magic.

The strategy and direction for data management starts in the boardroom. The leaders of the organisation need to show the required leadership and be accountable for it.

The essential allocation of time and resources, combined with the driving of the vital cultural change, can only be set by example at this level. Recognition that effective and efficient data management is actually a business optimisation strategy, and all that it implies, can only come from the very top of the organisation.

Yet how many Boards have an executive or non-executive director for data management? Why is the performance of data management not covered in annual reports like the rest of business?

Ingredients

Active shareholders

A competent board

Annual report

Include data management within balanced scorecard reporting

Instructions

1) Use active shareholders to force accountability of the board to shareholders for data management issues.

2) Appoint a director or non-executive director to be responsible for data management and to report to the board.

3) Include data management within annual report.

4) Data management performance reporting within balanced scorecards.

Seven Steps

Despite the protests of IT people, data management is not complicated. Data management starts at source in the business and only the most basic level of IT, if any, is required to achieve it.

We illustrate the principles of data management with the example of an internal phone directory. A CEO would never allow all employees to sit there on a regular basis reinventing company phone lists. The phone directory is produced using the seven basic steps of data management:

- **Accessions:** Data entering an organisation are monitored. The addition of new customers and the expiry of customers is tracked and managed.

- **Transfer:** All of the data are transferred into the format required for the directory – all the data put into one format.

- **Data Laundry:** Time is spent sorting out all the data to get a product.

- **Quality Control:** The names, addresses and numbers are checked by some mechanism.

- **Documentation:** The policies and procedures, quality control criteria and format specifications etc. relating to the phone directory are documented.

- **Banking the Data:** The data for the directory are archived and a hard copy of the directory is kept safely for future use.

- **Available to Users:** The directory is produced and distributed to customers.

Accessions

This is knowing what data you have and what is coming into an organisation so that it can be tracked. Consider this to be equivalent to a directory of employees in a company. This directory would contain a list of employees, contact details, who they report to, where they are, what they do etc. For the data it would include an inventory of data held, who is responsible, who has access, where it is located, etc.

Transfer

Data comes in to an organisation in a variety of formats and needs to be converted into organisational standards for inclusion within systems. Examples of this include the manual entry of faxed data for ordering or the submission of data into a request system from an online form.

Data Laundry

Data laundry, or data cleansing, is a key value-adding process and entails the sorting out of what's what. This can be part of the transfer and quality control procedures and is often a very time-consuming step. The process is all about taking data and cleaning it up to make it useful. An example could be an application for a driving licence where an officer would take a hastily written and incomplete application form, enter it into the system, check the validity of the entry, verify the credentials and check for duplicate applications.

Data laundry is one of the slowest and most frustrating steps. Too often its importance is overlooked and the time involved is usually NOT appreciated. Whilst data laundry is a cost, the costs associated with correcting it later are of a higher magnitude than doing it properly up front.

Quality Control

One of the most important steps in the process. The consequences of having incorrect data can result in significant financial losses, e.g. a $5 million currency transfer going to the wrong account, or court cases.

For different data types and systems, organisations should have a range of quality control checks. These checks need to be monitored and performance followed. It is the quality of the hand-off (transfer) between people and steps in a business process which ensures an effective and efficient business operation.

Documentation

Documentation is about trapping what has been done to the data, the policies and procedures, issues relating to the data and more. Without this documentation the data are of little use. Documentation is key to enhancing corporate expertise and allows others to pick up where one stops. It also makes the whole activity a replicable process. Documentation is one of the most important steps but is often overlooked.

Archiving

The need for data archiving (back up and recovery) is recognised but poor policies and procedures frequently exist. The ability to reconstruct to a set point in time is the measure of an effective system. Banking of data is not constrained to merely electronic media but includes records management and vouchered samples.

Making Information Available to Users

This is the final and most visible step. Whilst the rest of the system does not have to be attractive, only functional, this is where it is crucial to have the attractive interfaces. However, without the previous six steps, the most attractive interface is practically useless when the outcome is garbage.

Information Relationships

Information does not exist in isolation. We need to know how to link pieces of information together.

When entering a hotel room, many people like to see their favourite food or drink in the room. The hotel achieves this by linking the data about the customer to that of the visit, to that of their likes and dislikes – they manage the relationships between information.

It is not enough to manage data and information. Expertise and experience come from using separate pieces of information together, i.e. wisdom comes from knowing and using the relationships between information data and work-flow are tied.

Many businesses struggle to guarantee service delivery because the relationship information is not shared within the organisation.

Information relationship management comes from basic metadata (data that describes data). With a coherent, comprehensive and authoritative metadata framework, the returns from knowledge management are significantly increased.

Sustainable Simplicity

The key to data management is the simplicity of the solution and its sustainability.

Expectation Management

As long as the business is operating and creating new pieces of data and information, the need for knowledge management will continue. So will the costs and the needs for ever-improved performance.

Knowledge management is not a panacea and silver bullet that will magically solve all problems. Nor is it something that will just happen.

The big bang approach to knowledge management has been shown to be a failure. It is a slow ongoing process of progressive change, integrated into, and championed by, the business.

> **Have You Considered?**
>
> - Data management and business optimisation go hand in hand;
> - Data management is a way to drive cultural change;
> - Data management succeeds when it is driven at source and integrated into everyday business.

It is very important that the expectations of all people be realistic and that the expectations are managed.

Priority Management

In any discussion on the data management issue, a tendency exists for users to look at all the old tapes that can no longer be read and the stacks of computer printouts and – justifiably – feel overwhelmed. This does NOT need to be the case. A fundamental distinction needs to be drawn between the mountain of data that exists and putting in place a mechanism to manage data from this time forward: so stopping the accumulation of unmanaged data.

It is a case of "drawing a line in the sand" and managing data properly from this time forward. The mechanism can be simple, needing a small shift in political viewpoint and will take a little focused effort every now and then. One will then have the tools to chip away at the mountain that already exists, which will occur as priorities dictate.

Actionable Monitoring

A key component of the exercise is to monitor the activities, the benefits gained, the quality of the information and data management, the costs etc. It is not enough just to monitor. It has to be actionable monitoring. One of the challenges is to establish the hidden costs and inefficiencies of the status quo so that performances can be bench marked.

Communication

Successful knowledge and data management occurs when it is championed and adopted at the coalface (frontline). The business benefits must be seen on a daily basis at the coalface and the participants reminded of what it was like before.

Effective communication throughout the exercise is critical. This will not only cover what is planned and why but also the impacts and benefits. This will be an ongoing exercise.

Cultural Change

Knowledge and data management is about systems and processes to organise people who naturally tend to be disorganised. The adoption of these new ways of operating is a cultural change exercise. Cultural change is a slow and painful process. Whilst it is important to have some high profile wins and for progress to be seen, it is like an iceberg that suddenly appears. The nine-tenths below the waterline are what count and this is unseen and unappreciated.

Role of IT

IT systems have a lot to contribute to and play a critical role in effective and efficient data management. However, effective and efficient data management occurred long before IT systems, and significant performance gains can be achieved without any new IT solutions.

Recognition that IT is linked to, and driven by, information management and work-flow is a hallmark of successful knowledge management. The IT solution needs to be considered in the same context as parts management and an assembly line for the roles of knowledge workers.

Easy and Business Integrated

Successful data and knowledge management activities are not based around the big bang. The theory of "if people just did it this way then things would be fine" simply does not work. It has to be implemented at, and championed by, the coalface. Above all, the process has to be easy and done as a matter of course, as an integral part of everyday business.

Tantalising Technology

Information Technology (IT) is the assembly line for the knowledge workers. IT exists to service the needs of the business.

Information Technology (IT) is often sold and brought in as a panacea and a silver bullet. More technology is seen as the way to solve systemic business problems, and yet, as we all know, nothing could be further from the truth.

User cynicism with IT and its failed promises is at a record high. Such is the level of user discontent that users devise all sorts of ingenious ways to bypass IT departments. Others have just given up and believe that things cannot possibly get any worse, so let's try and outsource it.

The areas of failing are numerous and include:

> **Key Ingredients**
> - Accountability of IT to the Board, market and shareholders;
> - Treating IT as an assembly line for knowledge workers;
> - Rigorous business case and architecture;
> - Core competency to be kept in-house.

- budget blow-outs and project over-runs;
- total failure to deliver promised savings;
- disparate systems;
- duplication of effort and information;
- chasing moving goal posts;
- continuous upgrade cycle;
- poor outsourcing agreements.

Since IT exists to service the needs of the business, the failings of IT are ultimately failings of the business.

By looking at successful examples, the failings of IT can be avoided.

Technology alone is a high cost and ineffective operation (Figure 9). A successful operation can be achieved through information management and work-flow, but it tends to be high cost.

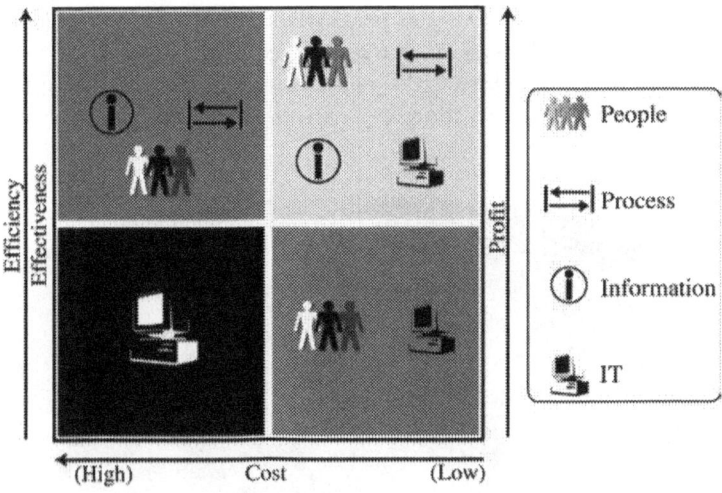

Figure 9. Alignment of people, process, information and IT.

It is the calibre of staff, together with information management and work-flow and IT, that creates a profitable, efficient and low cost operation.

Boardroom Balance

The failure of IT to deliver reflects the vision, strategy and accountability seen in the boardroom.

The strategy and direction for IT starts in the boardroom. The budget blow-outs, the failed implementations, the poor outsourcing deals etc. are ultimately the responsibility of the board. Yet how many boards have an executive or non-executive director for IT? Why is the performance of IT not covered in annual reports when all other areas of the business are?

The ongoing failure of IT is seen from Figure 10 where the majority of the spend allocated is invested in the hardware and software.

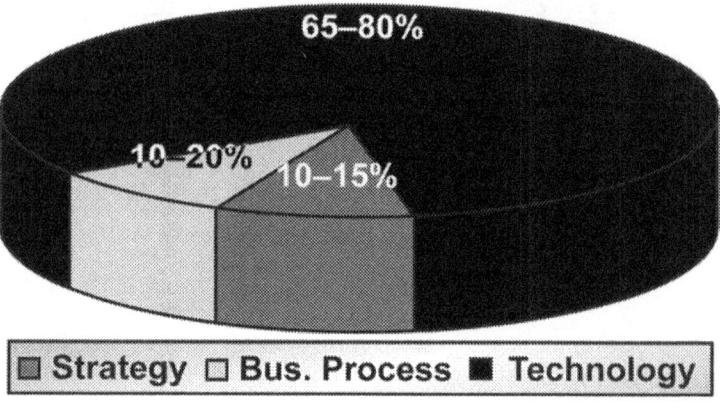

Figure 10. Current IT spend within projects in many organisations.

To deliver the required results, the majority of the money and effort should be spent on business issues and business integration (Figure 11).

Tantalising Technology

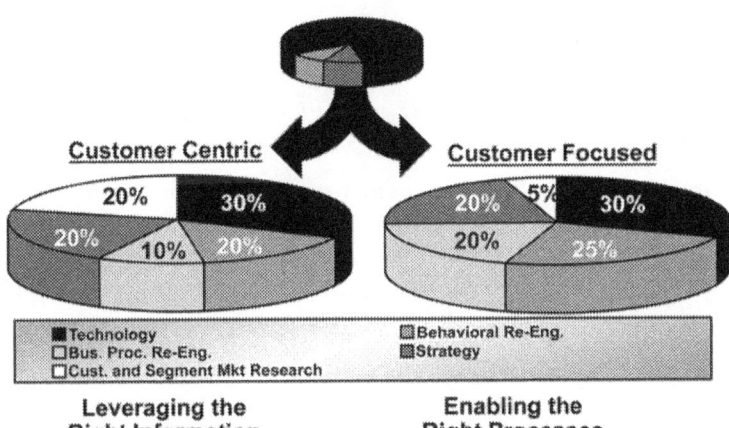

Figure 11. Appropriate IT spend to deliver results.

Ingredients

Active shareholders

A competent Board

Annual report

Disclosure to share market

Include IT within balanced scorecard reporting

Instructions

1) Use active shareholders to force accountability of the Board to shareholders for IT performance.

2) Appoint a director or non-executive director to be responsible for IT and to report to the board.

3) Quality-assure all IT outcomes at the board level.

4) Include IT performance within annual report.

5) IT performance reporting within balanced scorecards.

6) Disclosure of IT issues to share market.

Defining the Driver

Understand the basics: The business drives IT. IT does NOT drive the business. IT exists to meet the needs of the business.

The once-famous quote of a chief operations officer was "those damn bean counters cost us more money through lost clients than they save us!" seems to be as true as ever. Except that now it is the excesses of IT that gets the wrath of the chief operations officer.

The biggest complaints have revolved around:

- IT driving the business instead of the business driving IT;
- Chasing moving goal posts;
- Lack of business integration and failure to deliver.

Since many in the business are not in a position to understand IT and many in IT are the same when it comes to the business, a void between the two exists. With marketing hype and a hope for the panacea, IT is often driving the business instead of the business driving IT.

Ingredients

A business with clearly defined goals and objectives

Business resources who understand IT and its application from a holistic view

An IT department that understands that it should meet the needs of the business and is accountable to the business

Instructions

1) Take an area of the business that knows what it wants and is doing.

2) Have business people with an understanding of IT, who can explain the benefits to the business and show how IT can be applied.

3) Business develops needs and business case.

4) IT department services the needs of the business.

The IT Assembly Line

IT is a production line for knowledge workers to deliver results for customers. The production line needs to be designed from this perspective.

Whether it is an account balance or the sale of a product, knowledge workers take information from different sources, compile it, and present it back to customers in sequence. Each task is a recipe that is consistently repeated. The right information needs to be presented in the right way at the right time.

> **Productivity Principle**
>
> Manufacturing assembly lines are re-tooled only when product designs change and/or the tools are too old.
>
> What is the difference with a knowledge worker assembly line?

Yet if you look at many IT implementations, they appear to be purposely designed to complicate the role of knowledge workers and to impede the delivery of service.

Ingredients

Defined audience-task-recipes

Integrated work-flow and information requirement across the business

Optimised assembly line design

IT solution to deliver assembly line

Maintenance, monitoring and reporting

Instructions

1) For each audience, define the tasks and recipes across the enterprise.

2) Analyse and simulate the flow of information at each step and optimise.

3) Design assembly line to support business operation.

4) Implement IT solution to deliver production line.

5) Ongoing monitoring, reporting and maintenance.

A-grade Architecture

The same fundamental principles of engineering and design that are used for buildings, assembly lines and products apply to IT solutions.

When a building is constructed or an assembly line implemented, it is considered to be a large infrastructure investment designed to last many years.

For a building, a rigorous design and engineering process is completed in response to the requirements of legislation, the market trends, cost and customer needs (Figure 12). These same factors and design-engineering process drive product design in business and the resulting assembly line is developed to make the products.

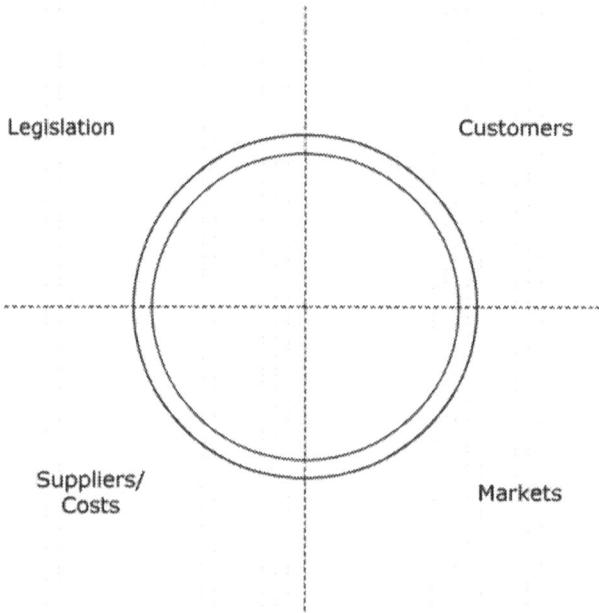

Figure 12. The drivers for IT architecture.

Contrast this approach and philosophy with that prevailing for IT and software development, where a rigorous design and engineering process is absent and IT is not considered as a mission-critical assembly line for knowledge workers which will need to function effectively for years.

It is interesting to note that once an IT solution is implemented, it is there for years, e.g. COBOL, developed in 1959, still runs many mission-critical corporate systems.

Ingredients	Instructions
Services to be provided by audience	1) Establish services to be delivered (define the product).
Parts for delivery of services	2) Map business processes as the audience interacts to meet customer needs.
Bill of materials for each service to be delivered	
Work-flow and recipes	3) Define required parts and bills of materials required to manufacture the services.
	4) Engineer recipes and model with work-flow simulation tools.
	5) Specify requirements.
	6) Design solution and implement in a phased way using proven business principles.

Consolidated Data Storage and Access

In the move from mainframes to PCs and the Internet, the benefits of managed information and work-flow have been lost.

The adoption of distributive computing power has been a good shift but there is a need to return to consolidated data/information storage and work-flow (Figure 13).

Without this, the sharing of knowledge and collaboration will continue to decline and user frustration and hidden costs keep on increasing. Current strategies within much of IT are serving to perpetuate this problem.

Ingredients	Instructions
Documents	1) Establish consolidated corporate repository that is accessible across the network.
E-mails	
Transactional data	2) Ensure all documents are stored in a document management system as part of the corporate repository.
Databases	
Spatial data	
Corporate repository accessible across network	3) All databases to be consolidated in the corporate repository.
	4) All transaction data to be consolidated in the corporate repository.
	5) Integrate e-mail storage into corporate repository.
	6) Educate personnel and implement the required carrots and sticks.

The adoption of distributed computing power is good but the gods in white coats of IT have left us with a most dangerous legacy – lack of consolidated data storage and work-flow. It will fall to the user to remedy the failings of IT.

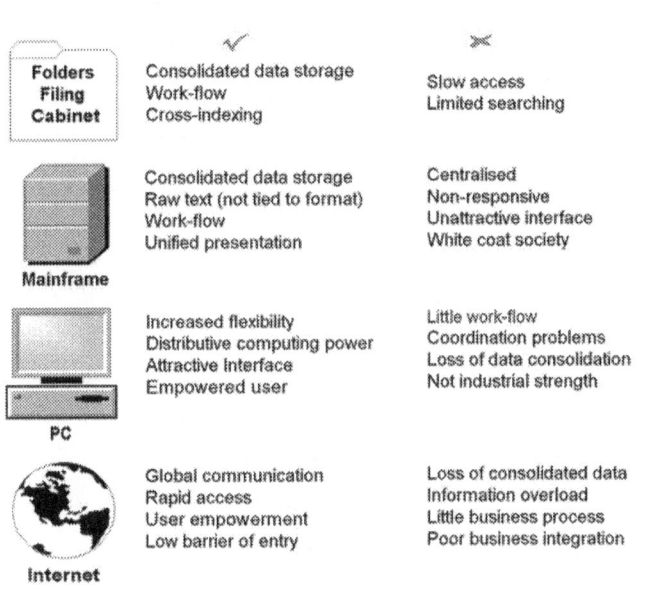

Figure 13. The dangerous legacy from IT.

Information Presentation and Delivery

Single source information by separating the information from its presentation and mechanism of delivery.

On an assembly line, different people perform different roles and don't need to worry about where the parts come from. The design of the assembly line ensures that they just get the right parts at the right time, i.e. the parts come to the people.

Contrast this with knowledge workers who need intimate knowledge of:

- where information is stored;
- what application the information is stored in;
- how to get the information;
- where to use it in the process.

What is even worse is that the knowledge workers:

- vary in their capabilities;
- go to the parts;
- collect the parts one at a time;
- create multiple instances of a part (copy and paste) when there should be no need to.

The resolution of the problem lies not only in the application of assembly line principles but in the separation of information from presentation and the mechanisms of delivery (Figure 14).

With information stored in a consolidated repository, separated from presentation and the mechanism of delivery, an effective and efficient IT infrastructure can be architected.

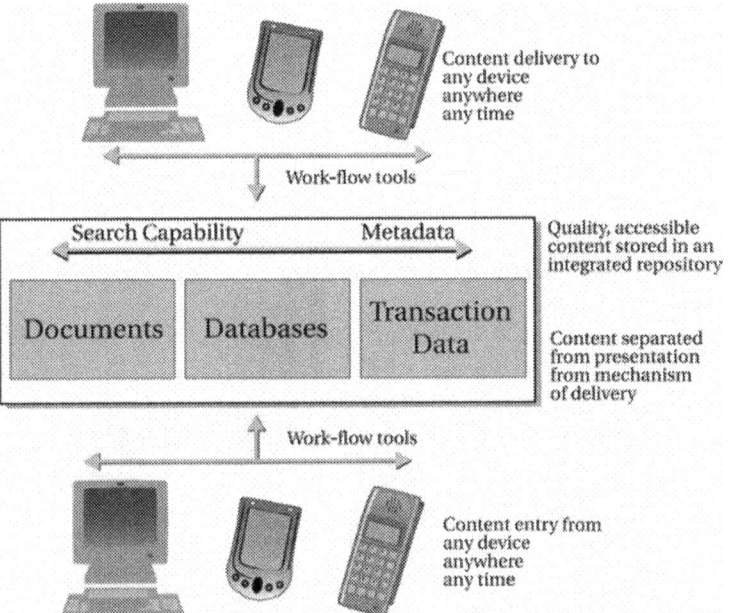

Figure 14. Information to and from any device, anywhere, any time.

Migration Mitigation

The cost of an IT solution is the cost of the IT plus the cost and pain to move.

IT is sold as a panacea and a silver bullet. If you only purchased this new feature it would solve this problem, and yet all of the evidence shows the contrary. Who is worse – the one that sells the panacea and the silver bullet or the one who buys it?

The cost to replace a system is not just the hardware and software; it is the cost to migrate (Figure 15). A new feature has to provide significant benefits and cost savings to cover the cost of migration.

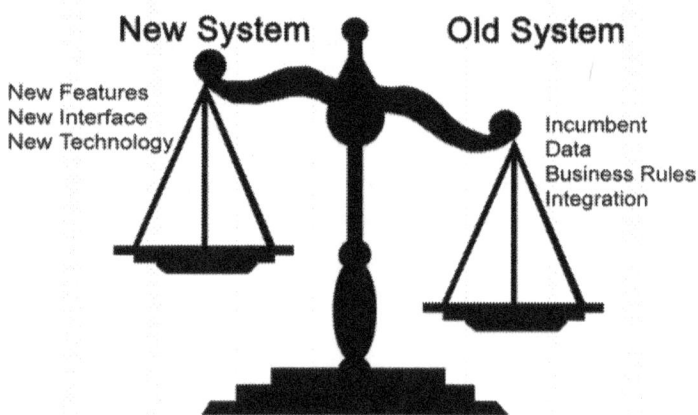

Figure 15. The real cost is the cost to move.

This inability to differentiate between the feature cost and the cost to migrate is one of the main reasons for the constant chasing of the moving goalposts and the resultant user frustration.

If the business does NOT drive a migration and does NOT spare the time and resources for it, then the incumbent system and problem cannot be that bad. Leave it alone!

Ingredients

Business to drive the need and migration

Comprehensive features and benefit analysis

Business case including full costing and return on investment

Quality and performance incentives and damages for both IT and the business

Detailed risk management plan to cover contingencies

Instructions

1) Establish that the pain associated with the incumbent system is so bad for the business that they will spend time away from core activities to fix it.

2) Conclude what-if and scenario modelling of the impacts of the change upon the assembly line.

3) Conduct extensive features and benefits analysis to cover return on investment for all aspects of the business under best- and worse-case conditions.

4) Establish risk management plan to cover contingencies.

5) Migrate system if appropriate.

Organised Outsourcing

Control of IT is a core competency that needs to be kept in-house.

IT outsourcing is now an everyday business occurrence and yet the failings are all too numerous.

- Since IT is intimately linked to information management and work-flow, why are they considered to be separate and IT outsourced in isolation?

- Most business people would agree that the ability to design, optimise, and repair an assembly line is a core competency that should be kept in-house. Why is IT outsourced?

- Whilst parts are sourced from multiple suppliers, a continuity in the design and operation of the assembly line is considered critical. By outsourcing IT you break up the continuity of the knowledge worker assembly line.

- Why does the expertise to design the assembly line for your knowledge workers reside with an outsourcer who does not know your business?

These and many more are reasons why IT is a core competency that should be kept in-house.

See Breaking the Relationship in Optimised Outsourcing to regain control of your knowledge workers, information management and work-flow and the required assembly line.

Precision Parts

Document management is a stepping stone to achieving the real goal of parts management.

An assembly line relies on parts management, bills of materials, and work-flow. Parts management is a proven activity and is pivotal to successful manufacturing. Thousands of parts are routinely ordered, inventoried, managed and assembled into other parts. The same principles apply to catering, cleaning and many other industries, yet the approach is alien to IT and the roles of knowledge workers.

Consider an invoice. This consists of a template, transactional data, a logo, business specific information, promotional information, billing details, terms and conditions etc. All of these are parts that are combined using a bill of materials to produce another part.

The same approach applies to documents, web pages, presentations, etc.

To have documents, databases and transactional data managed would be a significant achievement but the logical approach is to use parts management.

Internet Interactivity

Interactivity is the key significance of the Internet to business.

No discussion on business optimisation would be complete without mention of the Internet.

Many lessons have been learned from the wash-up of the Dot Coms. Not least of these is the importance of the Internet in optimising the role of knowledge workers. The key element of the Internet is interactivity and the ability to self-serve customers.

Whilst it is still early days, the ability to query online, to order online and to pay online is removing and changing the role of the knowledge workers. The ability to do these activities removes the need for operatives in call centres to answer queries and place orders. In addition, their role changes to problem resolution when things do not work.

> **Productivity Tip**
>
> Optimising a business around the Internet only works when proven business processes are brought to the Internet.

This trend of knowledge worker optimisation will continue as more and more processes go online. The key, however, will be the work-flow and information management necessary to support the activities.

Wondrous Websites

Websites work when they are customer centric, providing the work-flow necessary to achieve tasks.

Websites are moving from brochure-ware to mission-critical 24/7 business systems. In addition, they are becoming the focal point for all corporate knowledge, to be the conduit for business transactions, whilst simultaneously serving formal and informal communication needs within and between businesses.

> **Productivity Tip**
>
> The structure of websites is a series of linked proven business recipes.

The problem, however, is that the design of many websites is not geared towards this. Focusing on the view of the customer, then the website would reflect how the customer interacted with an organisation and not the category or internal structures currently seen on many brochure-ware sites (Figure 16).

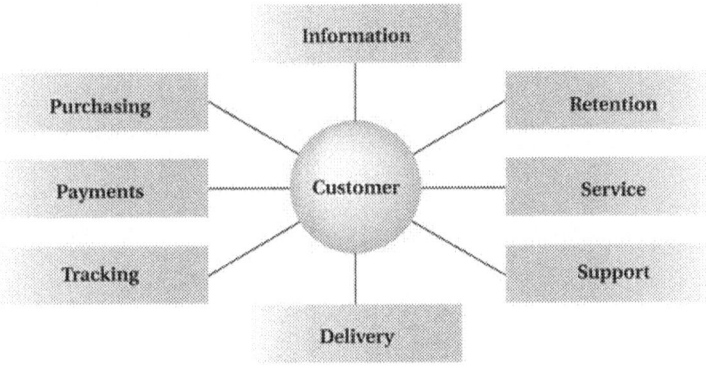

Figure 16. Customer-focused websites.

The design of the website moves from a series of browsing-based, vain searches for information to being a series of tasks that reflect proven business processes. These tasks vary according to the audience and provide the required information at each step of the process (Audience – Task – Recipe, ATR).

Ingredients

Identification of key business processes to be optimised around the Internet

Resolution of detailed recipes for key business processes

Access to all information required for the recipes without copying and pasting from back-office systems

Business integration of Internet

Instructions

1) After identifying key business processes, analysis for use and optimisation around the Internet.

2) Optimise recipes ensuring delivery of information at each step without the need to copy and paste from back-office systems.

3) Design website to reflect key recipes delivering information as required.

4) Provide informative navigation to link recipes.

5) Implement into the business with training and ensure that the customers and staff see the same recipes and interact accordingly.

Internet Integration

Benefits of the Internet come when it is integrated into business and NOT seen as an afterthought to business.

One of the major challenges with e-business has been the integration of websites and the Internet into everyday business practices. The Internet is still often seen as a different activity and an afterthought to many business activities, e.g. marketing campaigns.

The highly visual nature of websites makes them an ideal tool for driving business needs and business integration.

By designing websites:

- from the home page down, from a customer focus, you drive out the business need, business case and site structure;
- using business processes, both the required content and the navigation are resolved;
- using proven business processes you determine all of the back-office integration issues;
- in the business for the business, the sites are championed at source and owned at source;
- on the basis of business need, the required business integration is achieved;
- the visual aspects provoke an immediate impact and the consequences of decisions are seen.

Intranet – Internet Inclusion

An Internet and an Intranet presence are one. They are just different sides of the same coin.

In the early days, the Internet was considered as an equal source of information for all. It was only when this principle was no longer applicable and with the use of login IDs, did the need for Internets and Intranets arise. Within many organisations, information is duplicated between Internets and Intranets and between sites within them.

As websites become more aligned to business processes, the need for differences between Internets and Intranets will be reduced and access to information will be on the basis of role-based access.

The Audience – Task – Recipe (ATR) approach applies to all areas of business and to both internal and external customers.

When using ATR, a customer sees the same information and interacts the same as a customer service representative. In addition, the site navigation is simplified.

The metadata framework and the information relationship information are critical to the success of role-based access.

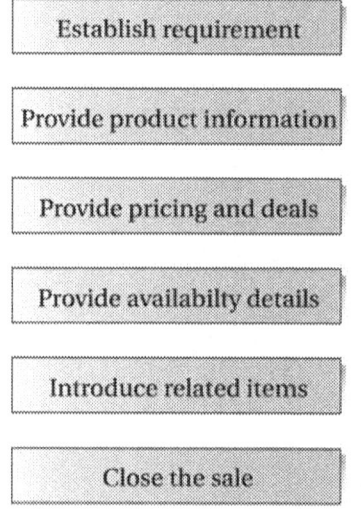

Figure 17. A recipe for the sales process.

Optimised Outsourcing

Outsourcing works well when it is done properly!

Since Kodak first outsourced its IT, outsourcing has become an important part of business and plays a valuable role within the modern corporate environment. Whilst there are many successes, the failures are also numerous. Whether it is the now infamous government outsourcing of IT services or TNT and the outsourcing of its administration, common failings are seen.

The way to successfully outsource and to fix the current outsourcing problems can be seen by looking at these mistakes.

> **Key Ingredients**
>
> - Keep strategy in-house;
> - Keep core competencies in-house;
> - Keep problem resolution in-house;
> - Keep ownership in-house;
> - Understand business processes and interaction;
> - Use incentive based outsourcing.

Securing Strategy

Business strategy is a core competency that needs to be controlled and set in-house.

Whether it is branding, marketing or IT, the history of business mediocrity is hallmarked by the outsourcing of strategy and the consequent loss of control and/or collapse of the business.

Consider IT outsourcing. Many deals include the provision of IT strategy. Given that IT is there to service the business need and that IT strategy comes from business strategy, why outsource IT strategy?

Given that the core competency of an outsourcer is not your business, why would they be experts in your strategy?

> **Key Ingredient**
>
> Keep control of the business by keeping problem resolution in-house and outsource the delivery where appropriate.

Ingredients

Business vision and strategy

Market understanding

Expertise from the outsourcer

Business subject matter expertise

Instructions

1) Combine business vision and strategy with market expertise and other business subject matter expertise.

2) Consult with outsourcer on their expertise.

3) Develop strategy and obtain details on implementation from outsourcer.

4) Alternatively sever strategy arrangement with outsourcer and keep in-house.

Preventing Problem Passing

Why is the passing of a problem to someone who has not been commissioned to fix it going to result in the problem being fixed?

There is a natural tendency for people to ignore problems and to pass them on to other people for resolution. This "problem passing" is rife within outsourcing, where whole business operations and critical areas of business are passed out in the vain hope that the outsourcer can fix undefined problems.

Since an outsourcer charges for services rendered, where is the incentive for them to change the status quo?

Ingredients

A non-core area of business

An understanding of business processes

Identification of interaction with other parts of the business

Quality of and recognition of hand-offs

Performance reporting and management

Instructions

1) Establish the business case for outsourcing a non-core area of business.

2) Map area of business in terms of a production line and define the inputs, outputs and quality of hand-offs.

3) Agree with outsourcer the parts and resources to be supplied, at what schedule, quality and price.

4) Integration of outsourcing supply into the production line.

5) Implement with strict monitoring and actionable managerial reporting, including quality and cost.

Owning Ownership

Lose ownership and you lose control!

Associated with "problem passing" is the reluctance of either the business or the outsourcer to take ownership of issues. In many arrangements, the blame is passed and there is an avoidance by either party to accept ownership.

Whilst many outsourcing relationships have account management, often just a mechanism for selling more services, a clear responsibility and procedure for problem resolution and escalation both within the business and the outsourcer is required. More importantly, a culture of proactive problem solving and responsibility is required.

Ingredients

A culture of proactive problem solving

Rewards for problem resolution and forfeits for perpetuation of the problem

Staff with defined roles to take ownership and work across boundaries to solve problems

Quality assured procedures for problem resolution and escalation

Performance reporting and management

Instructions

1) Structure support for staff, with defined roles to take ownership and problem solve, with the ability to work across business boundaries.

2) Using the culture of proactive problem resolution present within the business, align the outsourcer to the systems and practices.

3) Negotiate procedures, within the outsourcing arrangements for problem escalation and resolution.

4) Implement actionable managerial reporting.

Intellectual Property Intern

How much intellectual property is lost through outsourcing?

It is taken for granted that companies protect their intellectual property. Whether it be the signing of agreements or the management of human capital, any business discarding its intellectual property would be considered uninformed. Despite the obviousness, intellectual property is routinely lost in outsourcing agreements. Amongst other things, this results in escalating hidden costs and loss of control.

Ingredients

Cooperative outsourcer

Intellectual property protection agreements

Intellectual property performance agreements in outsourcing contracts

Knowledge capture and management regime

Regular transfer of expertise

Performance reporting and management

Instructions

1) With a cooperative outsourcer, establish the importance of intellectual property protection.

2) Negotiate intellectual property protection into outsourcing agreements.

3) Ensure adoption of the knowledge capture and management regime by outsourcer.

4) Regular and quality transfer of expertise from outsourcer to in-house resources.

5) Implement with strict monitoring and actionable managerial reporting, including quality and cost.

Accountant Accountability

Be sure that the costs associated with outsourcing are fully accounted for.

One of the main reasons cited for outsourcing is the lowering of costs. Whilst this has been successfully achieved, there are many instances where the true costs have not been considered and the promised savings have not been realised. Reasons for cost blow-outs include:

- lack of definition of, and accountability on, services to be provided;
- failure to understand business operation and processes and their interaction with the impact upon outsourcing;
- poor service provision by, and management of outsourcer;
- cutting back on lower paid resources, resulting in higher paid resources ineffectively using their time;
- artificial cost saving by using inferior resources.

Ingredients

An understanding of business processes and interactions

Business and scenario modelling

Financial management with operational expertise and understanding

Performance reporting and management

Instructions

1) For the area to be outsourced, model business processes and interactions.

2) Extensive what-if scenario modelling, allowing for variable outsourcer performance at key points.

3) Formalise outsourcing relationships on the basis of performance and cost.

4) Accountability within finance for operational failings as a result of outsourcing.

Business Process Bonds

One of the key reasons for outsourcing failures is a lack of understanding of what is being outsourced and a failure to distinguish between core and non-core competencies.

For a financial institution, catering and cleaning are non-core activities and are ideal for outsourcing. Transaction processing however, would be considered a core competency and outsourcing of this without fully understanding the business and its interaction with other areas of the business would have a significant impact upon business performance.

Although mentioned in passing in the other recipes, it is fundamental to outsourcing success that the business processes to be outsourced and their interactions be fully understood.

Ingredients

An understanding of business processes and how they operate

Identification of critical core competencies

Quality assurance of hand-off points

Performance reporting and management

Instructions

1) Review business processes that are proposed for outsourcing and eliminate core competencies from proposal.

2) Ascertain hand-off points within processes and where they interface with proposed outsourcer.

3) Establish criteria for quality assurance, including hand-offs, and particularly with proposed outsourced components.

4) If proceeding with outsourcing, implement performance reporting and management in agreement.

Reward-Based Returns

Reward outsourcers on the basis of why they were engaged, e.g. if used because cheaper than in-house – then pay them on the basis of cost saving realised.

One of the main reasons for outsourcing is the need to lower costs and the ability of an outsourcer to supply the services cheaper than they can be provided in-house. Yet few outsourcers are paid on a performance-based sales model.

Like sales people on a base plus commission, outsourcers should be paid a base plus a percentage of every cost saving they realise and a bonus for excellence of service. The more cost savings they achieve, the bigger the bonus, with penalties for under-performance and for poor quality of service.

> **Key Ingredient**
>
> An outsourcer has promised lower costs, so get them to put their money where their mouth is and pay by cost savings realised.

Ingredients

An outsourcer with your best interests at heart and prepared to put their money where their mouth is

Comprehensive performance analysis and reporting systems

Properly negotiated outsourcing agreements

Instructions

1) Negotiate payment based on quality of services and cost savings realised agreement with outsourcer.

2) Share results from reporting system to ensure optimal relationship.

Dependency Through Empowerment

The more you empower people, the more reliant they become on you.

A major challenge faced with outsourcing is management of the relationship. Once a core competency is outsourced, e.g. IT, there is a tendency for the initiator to lose control of that part of the operation, i.e. the outsourcer becomes the controlling party.

This unfortunate trend flies in the face of proven business wisdom. The more you try to control a party, the greater the resistance and the worse the relationship becomes. The greater the freedom provided and the more you empower someone, the more reliant they become upon you, e.g. our total freedom to use electricity but our total dependence upon it. This lack of empowerment and the outsourcer dependency is one of the main reasons for failings of outsourcings.

> **Key Ingredient**
>
> A smart outsourcer will realise more value from a client by empowering them.

Ingredients

An agreement with outsourcer to skill up in-house resources to work alongside outsourcer

Procedures and expertise to manage projects from other resources alongside the outsourcer

Regular transfer of expertise from outsourcer to business

Instructions

1) Negotiate agreement with outsourcer to skill up in-house resources.

2) Provide in-house resources (employed by business) to work alongside outsourcer in key roles.

3) Ensure regular transfer of expertise from outsourcer to business.

Breaking the Relationship

Regaining control of your business makes sense and feels great!

Once the business has lost control and the relationship with the outsourcer becomes stretched and/or has broken down what does the business do? Break the cycle of outsourcer dependency

Like an alcoholic, it is easier to stay with the status quo, take short cuts and false starts. Eventually they will do it right and be better for it.

Ingredients	Instructions
Recognition of the problem	1) Recognise the problem and be at the point where to keep the outsourced status quo is worse than the pain to fix the problem.
Willingness to endure the pain for the good of the business	
Time	2) Take strategy in-house.
Budget	3) Progressively take work away from the outsourcer, skilling up in-house along the way.
	4) Initiate new projects without the outsourcer.
	5) Endure the process of attrition to the point that the outsourcer is not making enough money from you that you can break the agreement without being sued.

Best served cold, and savour the rewards of being back in control of your business.

Forward to the Future

The only thing provided by a big bang is damage to the business. Moving forward begins with the first step and is an ongoing journey of fulfilment.

Designing and implementing a production line for knowledge workers is a significant activity and the change may seem daunting.

Now, get real. The big bang and the vain hope that it would all work if only one particular method were followed, is doomed to fail. Yes, if you are starting from scratch then it may work but most people are not in that position.

Like all great things, the journey begins with the first small step and there is no panacea or silver bullet, rather an exciting journey of fulfilment and rewards for effort.

Sound business practice shows that a way to move forward is:

- Make the decision to move forward;
- Take responsibility for the decision;
- Using one area of business, conduct a pilot project by establishing the recipes and modelling the processes from end-to-end as seen by the customer;
- Assess the outcomes;
- Design the assembly line and implement;
- Assess the outcomes;
- Progressively implement across other areas of business.

Keep it simple and pragmatic.

Remember, people have an infinite capacity to creatively bypass systems that do not work for them. In addition, few people persist with systems that do not work for them – they simply stop using them.

www.ingramcontent.com/pod-product-compliance
Lightning Source LLC
Chambersburg PA
CBHW020454220526
45464CB00002B/988